MASSAGE

MADE EASY

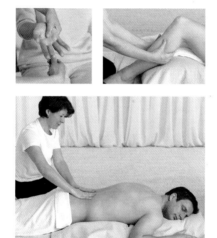

Joanna Trevelyan

Haldane **Mason**

First published in the UK in 2000 by Haldane Mason Ltd

This edition published for Boots plc in 2003 by
Pan Macmillan Ltd, 20 New Wharf Road, London N1 9RR

ISBN: 1-902463-20-X Haldane Mason
ISBN: 1-283063-83-1 Pan Macmillan

A HALDANE MASON BOOK

Editors: Jean Coppendale, Anne Hildyard, Beck Ward
Design: Louise Millar
Models: Carole-Ann Goodman, Nicola Mace, Paul Barrass, Keith Miller

Colour reproduction by CK Litho Ltd, UK

Printed in China

Picture Acknowledgements
All photographs by Sue Ford, with the exception of the following:
e.t.archive: 5; Andrew Sydenham: 13; Amanda Heywood: 57

IMPORTANT

The information in this book is generally applicable but is not tailored to
specific circumstances or individuals. The author and publishers can accept no
responsibility for any problems arising from following the information given in
this book. Safety information is supplied which should be read before
attempting to give a massage. Any of the oils can produce an allergic reaction.
If in doubt about any of the techniques described, please consult your doctor.

Contents

Massage

Introduction

Touch is one of the earliest senses we develop and we have put its healing properties to good use. If a part of our body aches, the natural reaction is to rub it gently to relieve the pain and tension. From such small beginnings therapeutic massage developed.

The history of massage remains largely unwritten but we do know the Chinese were using it as far back as 3000 BC. Massage is mentioned in the *Nei Jing* – a collection of books on Chinese medicine written around 400 BC the Indian *Ayur Veda* medical texts which date back to 1800 BC, and in ancient writings from Egypt, Japan and Persia.

The first written records of massage in the West date back to ancient Greece. Hippocrates, for example, called massage 'anatripsis' and wrote of its value in relieving muscular tension and improving muscle tone. Galen, who practised medicine in the 2nd century AD, recommended massage to the gladiators of Pergamum before and after exercise – something we now know reduces the risk of injury by warming and loosening up the muscles.

By the Middle Ages massage had decreased in popularity, as spiritual matters took precedence. But by the 16th century, however, massage had returned to favour and took a big leap forward in the 19th century when a Swedish professor, Per Hendrik Ling (1776–1839), developed a scientific system of massage based on what he had seen in China.

Swedish massage soon became popular throughout Europe and America, and was regularly prescribed by physicians and surgeons. During both World Wars massage was used in the rehabilitation of shell-shocked and injured soldiers, and nurses were trained in massage techniques well into the 20th century. However, as the wonders of high technology medicine captured the imagination of doctors, its use slowly declined.

More recently, complementary therapies such as massage have enjoyed another renaissance; as many as one in three people now use some form of complementary therapy as a regular part of their lifestyle.

Scene in a 16th-century Indian bath house showing one of the earliest records of head massage.

What is massage?

Massage involves the therapeutic manipulation of the soft tissues of the body – the muscles and ligaments. The manual techniques involved also have an effect on the circulatory, lymphatic and nervous systems.

Therapists use massage to ease tensions and knotted tissue, to increase the circulation of the blood and to stimulate the lymphatic system. After an injury, massage is used to break down adhesions and rebuild strength and mobility. And as anyone who has experienced massage will attest, it is wonderfully relaxing.

What better way to treat yourself after a hard day coping with the stresses and strains of modern life than to ease them away through a relaxing, invigorating, or sensuous massage?

MASSAGE CAN HELP WITH:

- stress and stress-related conditions such as insomnia, headaches, and backache due to muscle spasm
- high blood pressure
- arthritic and rheumatic pain
- mild symptoms of asthma
- colds
- constipation
- mild depression
- muscular strain and other sports injuries
- sciatic pain
- oedema
- cramps

Massage is also a health-promoting therapy, improving muscle tone, reducing muscular atrophy, helping people recuperate after illness. Some therapists claim regular massage will improve eyesight and hearing and lessen signs of ageing. Massaging babies helps them to relax and can alleviate problems such as colic, constipation and colds.

TYPES OF MASSAGE

Most types of massage use the techniques of Swedish massage which are explained later on in this book. The essential difference between the various types of massage is one of emphasis.

In the 19th century, emphasis was placed on the physical benefits of massage, where the techniques employed were often rather vigorous. Victorian massage manuals certainly did not mention that massage could be pleasurable or sensuous – this would have been viewed with disapproval, and not seen as a fashionable or acceptable notion in the slightest.

Today there is much greater emphasis on the agreeable aspects of massage and its powers of relaxation.

These newer forms of massage are often described as intuitive or holistic.

With intuitive massage the emphasis is on getting in touch with the tensions and emotions of the person being massaged (the receiver). Holistic massage places the therapy within a holistic framework and aims to have a psychological and spiritual effect as well as a physical one.

Gerda Boyesen, a Norwegian psychologist, physiotherapist and Reichian analyst, developed another type of therapeutic massage called biodynamic massage. The idea here is that the body can resolve emotional traumas and shocks if it is helped through massage to get rid of what Boyesen called 'patterns of chronic tension and psychological blocks'.

RESEARCH INTO MASSAGE

While most people who have experienced a massage talk about how relaxing and beneficial it can be, there is actually very little good quality research into the therapeutic benefits of massage. Every day thousands of people receive a massage, but in most cases only the receiver knows how effective it was, and not always immediately.

We do know that touch generally is beneficial and there is research that shows massage can affect blood and lymph flow, reduce muscle tension and increase musculo-skeletal flexibility. There is also research that indicates massage can reduce anxiety. For premature babies and babies that have a low birth weight, a gentle form of massage can be of great benefit.

Massage in health care

Here are a few examples of how massage is regularly used successfully within your health service:

- Patients with anorexia are offered massage to help encourage a more positive body image.
- Clinically depressed adolescents receiving a daily back massage feel less depressed and sleep better than those who watch relaxing videos.
- Stressed-out city office workers who receive an 'on-site' 10-minute massage feel invigorated and relaxed afterwards.
- People with cerebral palsy find abdominal massage an effective treatment for constipation.
- Patients undergoing radiotherapy treatment who receive a 10-minute massage have less symptom distress, tension and tiredness and a greater sense of vitality and tranquillity than patients who rest for 10 minutes.

The function of this book is to introduce you to the wonder of massage and to show you how to give a massage treatment safely and effectively. Cautionary guidelines are included which highlight important safety advice and provide a list of circumstances where a massage should not be given.

A section on preparation offers practical tips for preparing your massage space, yourself, and the receiver; it also includes suggestions for suitable music. Techniques are explained in full, showing you the basic movements and styles that are involved, as well as offering suggestions for practice.

Giving a Full Body Massage takes you step-by-step through massaging the entire body. It also gives step-by-step guidelines for a simple neck and shoulder massage to a receiver who is clothed, and a simple hand and foot massage for use any time, anywhere. In addition, advice is given on massaging in pregnancy and childbirth as well as for massaging babies and children.

Self massage is a very good way of perfecting general techniques with the added benefit that, at the same time, you are treating yourself. Various simple and quick self-massage techniques for stress relief and relaxation are explained, along with techniques to help with backache and headaches.

Finally, Using Essential Oils for Massage introduces you to the increasingly popular use of these oils in complementary medicine, and how they can enhance the effectiveness of the massage techniques you have learnt.

Perhaps the last word on the effectiveness of massage should go to Patricia McNamara, coordinator at the Wandsworth Cancer Support Centre, UK. What she has to say about massage for people with cancer is true also for people with many other conditions.

In 1994 Ms McNamara undertook a comprehensive survey into massage. Her conclusion was that: 'Therapeutic massage done in a gentle way is an ideal means of communicating care and compassion, nurturing the body and the whole person, helping breathing to deepen, muscles to let go of tension, reducing anxiety and of helping the person to befriend their body again. It also has the capacity to release energy by putting people in touch with the strong emotions evoked by the experience of having cancer, which are often suppressed in order to get through the treatment, or to protect the person's family from their anger, depression, fear or grief.'

With such a recommendation for massage, there really is little reason why you shouldn't feel able to try massage out for yourself, or to sit back and enjoy the benefits of being a receiver.

A 19th-century Japanese masseur: the benefits of massage have long been recognized in many different cultures.

Cautionary Guidelines

When given properly, massage is safe, relaxing and health-giving. However, it is important to be aware of safety issues. It may not be appropriate to offer a massage and this section will outline the circumstances when this applies. This section provides a checklist of safety issues for you and the receiver and questions to ask before massaging.

Massage is easy to learn, and if simple guidelines are followed, it is also safe.

SAFETY TIPS FOR YOU
- only massage if you are feeling well
- wear comfortable loose-fitting clothes that will not restrict your movements, remove your watch and any jewellery and cut your nails to avoid scratching
- wear comfortable shoes or go barefoot
- ensure you will not be disturbed; put the answer machine on and ask anyone in your home to be quiet

SAFETY TIPS FOR THE RECEIVER
Before massaging check that the receiver is warm and comfortable and has:
- no reasons for not being massaged
- no allergies to essential oils
- any positions they cannot lie or sit in
- been to the toilet beforehand
- removed jewellery, glasses and contact lenses
- not eaten for two hours
- not drunk alcohol or take non-prescription drugs beforehand

REMEMBER THE FOLLOWING
- always start and end with slow stroking movements
- scar tissue, varicose veins, bruising, tender or inflamed areas and sites of recent fractures should not be massaged directly
- do not massage for too long – a full body massage takes no more than one and a half hours

- do not massage one area for too long, to avoid tissue damage
- after a massage cover the receiver warmly and let them rest for a while and re-orient themselves

SAFETY IN THE MASSAGE SPACE

Before you start ensure:
- your space is warm and clean
- there is nothing you could trip over, or which could fall on the receiver
- equipment is in good working order
- you have enough oil, towels and pillows
- you keep your massage oils in a sealed bottle when not in use and always keep them out of the reach of children

WHEN NOT TO MASSAGE

A massage should not be given if the receiver has:
- an infectious disease (including skin diseases)
- a fever
- an acute inflammation
- a serious health problem such as heart disease or thrombosis
- recently undergone surgery
- any unexplained lumps or bumps
- acute undiagnosed back pain

If the receiver is in the first trimester of a pregnancy, do not massage. If the receiver is in a latter stage of pregnancy, always check with her doctor that massage is safe and if you should avoid certain areas of the body.

QUESTIONS TO ASK BEFORE GIVING A MASSAGE

- Do you have any serious health problems or infectious diseases, or have you undergone surgery recently?
- Do you have a temperature?
- Are you pregnant? If yes, check by how many months.
- Have you eaten or taken any medication within the last two hours?

If the answer is yes to any of the questions, then you should not give a massage.

You may also want to ask if the receiver has any other concerns that may be important to know about. Depending on the answer, you may decide a massage is inappropriate.

Preparat
AND
Techn

To give a really effective massage it is important to be well prepared and to have learned some of the basic techniques. The first part of this section will show you how to set the scene for a perfect massage, while the second part explains some of the basic movements and benefits to be had from them. This section will help you to:

- organize your massage space
- make the receiver feel comfortable
- prepare yourself physically, mentally and emotionally
- explain the basic techniques
- outline the benefits of each technique
- offer suggestions for practice

on
echnique

Preparing your space

Creating a comfortable, calm and relaxing setting does not require a special massage room. Any space can be transformed as long as it is tidy, clean, heated and draught free.

Soft, subdued lighting can be created by changing the colour of the light bulb in your overhead lighting (the colours for a relaxed atmosphere include pale pink, blue, green, peach or lavender) or by using table lamps and candles. Make sure candles are placed safely and that they are large enough to last throughout the massage.

A final touch is a pleasant fragrance; fresh flowers, incense or a bowl of potpourri can all provide an instant lift. Alternatively, try adding a few drops of essential oil to a bowl of water set on a radiator. This also ensures the atmosphere is not too dry. Otherwise try an essential oil burner.

EQUIPMENT

Massage can be given on the floor or a massage table. When massaging on the floor you will need to create a comfortable space. If you have carpets, a sleeping bag, a duvet or a couple of blankets laid out and covered with a towel will probably be enough. On harder surfaces you will need a little extra padding. Make sure the surface is wide enough for you to kneel on while massaging, otherwise your knees are likely to get rather sore.

Anyone who intends to do a lot of massage might consider investing in a massage table, available from medical supply companies. This will allow you to massage without bending and kneeling. Beds are rarely the right place to massage as they are usually too soft and too wide.

You will also need plenty of cushions to make the receiver comfortable, and towels to cover parts of the body not being massaged.

While it is not necessary to use oil when massaging, it does increase the effectiveness of the massage, allowing your hands to move smoothly over the body and preventing skin abrasions. The carrier oil or base oil that you choose should be of vegetable origin, cold pressed (not removed by chemicals), unrefined and additive free. Such oils are easily absorbed and contain vitamins, minerals and fatty acids that are good for the skin. You can either use one light oil, such as sunflower, grapeseed, sweet almond, or soya oil; or you can blend a lighter oil with a small amount of a thicker oil such as apricot kernel and peach kernel, avocado pear, calendula, evening primrose, jojoba or wheatgerm. You can also buy a specially prepared massage carrier oil.

MUSIC AND MASSAGE

Some people like a peaceful, quiet atmosphere when they are being massaged, others enjoy music in the background. Ask the receiver what they would prefer. Suggest they bring along a tape, or have a selection ready for them to choose from. There is no definitive list of appropriate music as everyone's taste is different. You can buy tapes with specially created music and sounds that are supposed to be relaxing, but these are not to everyone's taste. The important thing is that the music used is sympathetic to the atmosphere you have created.

Preparing yourself

As well as choosing the right clothes to wear and being in good health, it is also important to prepare your hands for the work they are about to do. They need to be both supple and sensitive, and there are several ways you can develop this.

1 Hold a small rubber ball and alternate squeezing it and relaxing your hand.

2 Hold your hands together. Lift your elbows until your palms no longer touch, and press your fingers together.

3 Take each finger in turn, gently rotate and stretch. With your hands relaxed, circle both wrists clockwise and anticlockwise.

4 Throw out your fingers so that they are separated.

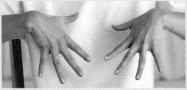

To increase the sensitivity of your hands, bring them together without actually touching. Repeat this,

gradually increasing the distance they move apart. Make a note of what you feel while doing this exercise – such as tingling or pulsating sensations or even a sense of heat or magnetism.

Sit opposite a friend with your hands about 5 cm (2 inches) away from their body. Starting with the head, move your hands slowly down the body. Repeat with your hands farther away. You should feel similar sensations to the previous exercise.

Now ask your friend to rest an arm on a table. Place your hand lightly on their forearm, focus your attention on the arm and note what you feel. You may feel drawn to particular parts of the arm, only to find that they may be the sites of past injuries.

Using your body properly while massaging will prevent damage to your back or knees, as well as preventing them from aching while you work. Keep your back straight, feet apart and knees bent if you are working on a table. Have your knees apart if you are working on the floor. Do not remain in one position for too long and try to make sure you face in the direction of your massage strokes.

Breathing is also important while massaging. Correct breathing means breathing in slowly over a count of three or four and feeling your abdomen expand. As you slowly breathe out, you should feel calmer and any tension should be released.

Lastly, you need to be relaxed and focused; take time to clear your mind. Sit quietly, take a few deep breaths and think about the person you will be massaging.

While massaging, you should be calm with your attention focused on the receiver. Be aware of their breathing and their reactions to what you are doing.

Preparing the receiver

When massaging only the hands, feet, shoulders or neck, it is not necessary for the receiver to undress. They simply need to sit or lie in a position that is comfortable.

For a full body massage it is easier if the receiver is naked, but underwear may be kept on if preferred. Make sure the receiver is warm and that any part of the body not being massaged is covered. Long hair should be comfortably secured away from the massage area.

Suggest the receiver closes their eyes, focuses on their breathing and lets go of any worries. They should allow their limbs to be moved without helping you. Remind the receiver to tell you if they are uncomfortable, cold or if the pressure being used is not right. Also suggest that any conversation is kept to a minimum.

Techniques

No massage is like another; each is as individual as the people involved. Yet whatever the style – brisk and invigorating or slow and relaxing – there are some basic techniques that need to be learned.

EFFLEURAGE (STROKING)

Effleurage is the most basic movement and is the one you will use the most to:
- make or break contact with the receiver
- spread oil
- massage any part of the body
- find tense areas
- link other massage movements
- make the whole body feel part of the massage experience

Use effleurage slowly to relax, reassure and sedate, or more briskly to revive and stimulate.

1 Start with your hands placed side by side. Glide them slowly upwards, fingers leading. To apply pressure, lean your body on to your hands.

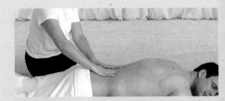

2 Glide your hands away from each other sliding gently down the side of the area being massaged. On this downward stroke no pressure should be applied.

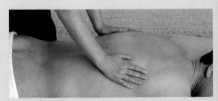

3 Bring your hands up the sides of the body, moulding into the curves. Move your hands back to the starting position, again exerting no pressure.

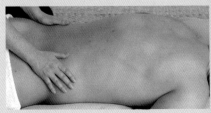

CIRCLING

Place both hands on one side of the body, about 15 cm (6 inches) apart, then stroke round in wide curves, making a circle. When your hands meet lift one hand over the other hand. Pressure should only be exerted on the upward strokes.

FEATHERING

Use your fingertips to brush lightly over the area concerned. Stroke down with one hand while the other is still. At the end of the stroke lift your hand back to the original position while at the same time beginning another stroke with the other hand.

GENERAL GUIDELINES FOR ALL TECHNIQUES

- Your movements should always be rhythmic.
- Vary the pressure according to what feels right.
- Use gentle pressure on tense or lumpy areas; deeper pressure will hurt the receiver and increase the tension.
- Massage should be pleasurable, so listen to what the receiver wants.
- If you tickle the receiver, try increasing the pressure or move to another area; as they become relaxed the ticklishness disappears and you will be able to massage the area again.
- Keep one hand in contact with the receiver's body; when you need more oil, pour a little on the hand touching the receiver, then place your other hand on top to smoothly transfer the oil onto the body.
- Remain focused on what you are doing and avoid general conversation.

19

DEEPER PRESSURE STROKES

These are also called petrissage *which is derived from the French* pétrir, *meaning 'to knead'.*

BASIC KNEADING

Place both hands on the body with fingers pointing away and elbows sticking out. Press down with the palm of one hand, grasp the flesh and push it towards the other hand.

Release the flesh and then grasp it with your other hand. As before, bring it towards the hand that has just released it. This alternating movement should be rhythmic and smooth.

THUMB PRESSURE

Using your thumbs to apply deep, direct pressure is an effective way of dealing with tense muscles. Put your thumbs on the body supported by the rest of your hand, then slowly lean into them to apply pressure. Release, and slide your thumbs to the next area. While you are exerting pressure you can also make slow circling movements with your thumbs.

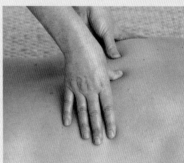

KNUCKLING

For knuckling, make your hands into loose fists and ripple your fingers round in small circular movement, applying your knuckles to the body.

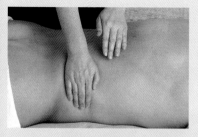

PULLING UP

Place your hands flat on the body and grasp the muscle rather than the skin, then pull it as far away as possible from the bone (without hurting the receiver).

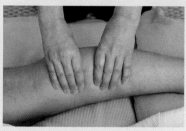

WRINGING

Here you need to imagine you are wringing a towel. Start with a basic kneading movement, then pull the flesh up and across towards your other hand. Use the thumb of that other hand to press deeply into the flesh.

USE DEEPER PRESSURE STROKES TO:

- relax muscles
- improve blood and lymphatic circulation
- help break up and dispose of waste products
- help break down the knots which build up as a result of stress
- offer temporary pain relief by increasing the temperature, cellular activity and blood flow in the affected area
- prevent muscle stiffness after exercise and relieve muscle spasm (particularly petrissage)
- work on bony parts and joints
- relax the soft fleshy parts of the body

PRACTISE TIPS

- Work deeper and deeper into the tissues gradually and make sure the pressure you use is acceptable to the receiver.
- Do not work on any one area for too long or it will get sore.
- Remain relaxed – hunching your shoulders will leave you in need of a massage.
- Make sure you are moving the tissues under the skin and not just the skin, otherwise you might accidentally pinch the receiver.

PERCUSSION

Also called tapotement, *these movements are light and brisk, applied with alternate hands in rapid succession as striking actions on the fleshy, muscular areas of the body.*

CUPPING

Form a hollow curve with your hands and with your palms facing down, bring them down on the body alternating one hand with the other.

A vacuum should be created and then released as you move your hands up. The sound made is much like a horse trotting.

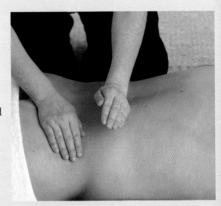

HACKING

Hold your hands over the receiver with the palms facing each other, thumbs uppermost. Then flick your hands up and down from the wrists in rapid succession (alternating one with the other), touching the body with the edge of your hand.

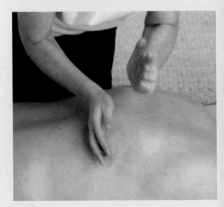

PUMMELLING

Make your hands into loose,
relaxed fists and bounce the side
of your fists lightly on the skin.

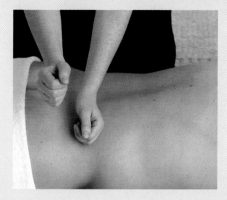

USE PERCUSSION TO:

- improve circulation, muscle tone and strength
- stimulate the body
- help reduce fat deposits and flabby muscle areas
- finish a massage and wake the receiver up; if you are trying to send your receiver to sleep – omit percussion movements
- prepare athletes before exercise
- combat constipation when applied to the abdomen

Cupping can loosen mucus in the lungs, aiding expectoration if used over the upper and middle back area

PRACTISE TIPS

- Try percussion on yourself first to get the pressure right, it should be light and bouncy rather than heavy and pounding.
- Do percussion movements over a towel to avoid hurting the receiver.
- Relax while doing these movements or you can lose the rhythm.
- Keep your hands, fingers and wrists relaxed and loose, elbows close to your body.
- Make sure your movements come from your wrists.
- Avoid the bony areas of the body as percussion will hurt these areas.
- When cupping, make sure your hands really are cupped, if they are not you will hear a smacking sound, possibly hurting the receiver.

Giving a

FULL

O nce you have mastered the basic techniques it is time to put them together in a full body massage. Practising with a friend can be great fun and beneficial for both of you. This section offers step-by-step guidelines for:

- full body massage
- neck and shoulder massage with the receiver clothed
- hand or foot massage with the receiver clothed

The sequences described are for guidance; select techniques that you feel confident about. Allow about ten minutes for each routine, plus a little more for the back. Remember to keep one hand in contact with the receiver so that you move smoothly from one area of the body to the next.

Body
MASSAGE

The Back

There is nothing quite like a deeply relaxing back massage, which gives the whole body a sense of well-being. Take your time, and most people will enjoy the experience.

Kneel next to the receiver's waist. Put oil on your warmed hands and place them on the lower back. Point your fingers towards the head and place thumbs each side of the spine. Spend a few moments relaxing and breathing.

Effleurage smoothly and rhythmically, using your body weight to apply pressure. Stroke over the whole back and shoulder area, following the body's contours. Then try some circular stroking movements.

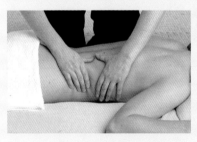

Kneading is excellent for the back. Face across the body and start from the lower back working up to the shoulders and neck. Knead the hips and up the sides of the body as well. Vary the pressure and the speed but keep your movements rhythmic.

To finish, relax your hands and stroke up the sides of the body, alternating your hands.

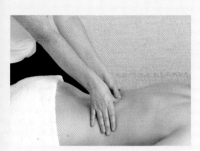

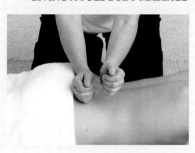

Use thumb pressure to work up the sides of the spine – keep your elbows straight while exerting pressure. Also try some circling thumb movements.

Place one hand on each side of the waist with fingers facing away from the spine. Pull the hand furthest from you up the side of the body towards you, while the hand nearest to you moves up the side and away from you. Pull up firmly and then glide gently over the back.

Use pummelling to invigorate – starting from the buttocks. Avoid the kidney area and the spine itself.

Complete with light effleurage and rest your hands on the small of the back for a moment.

Using alternate hands, start from the neck and feather down the spine gently. As one hand finishes, start with the other. Keep your movements rhythmic and slowly make the strokes lighter and lighter. Then stroke lightly down each side of the spine using your fingertips.

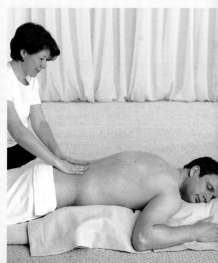

Neck and shoulders

A little extra work in this area can pay dividends in terms of relaxation, as we carry considerable tension here. Rest the head to one side, or face down with the forehead on a rolled towel.

Kneel with one knee up so you can apply extra pressure with your body.

Place your hands on each shoulder and effleurage up to the sides of the neck, applying pressure on the upwards stroke.

Knead along the shoulders up to the base of the skull.

Apply circling thumb pressure to the shoulders and neck.

Complete with effleurage over the whole back, shoulders and neck. Cover the shoulders and upper back with a towel using one hand, keep the other hand resting on the lower back.

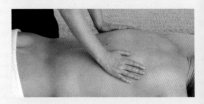

Buttocks

The muscles here are the most powerful in the body and can get very tense. Massage will help unlock tension and keep the buttocks in shape.

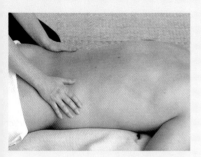

Kneel next to the buttocks and use circling effleurage on each side. Massage in a clockwise direction on the right side and in an anti-clockwise one on the left side. You can also use general effleurage.

Place both hands on the top of the buttocks to start. Stroke up and out, then down the waist and pull up firmly over the buttocks.

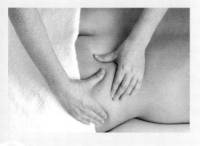

Applying firm pressure strokes such as kneading and circular pressure can really help relieve tension.

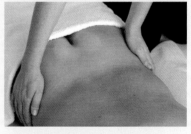

Bring both hands up the waist and finish with vigorous vibration. Place one hand over the top of the buttocks and vibrate the entire area rapidly, without pressure. Cover with a towel.

29

Legs

Massaging the legs helps to prevent varicose veins and is a good way to combat fatigue.

Before asking the receiver to turn over on to their back, massage the backs of their legs with effleurage from the ankles to thighs, using gentle pressure over the backs of the knees. Use thumb pressure over the calves.

Knead firmly up the thigh and pummel the outer thigh. Effleurage the whole leg, then lift up the foot, supporting it with one hand and using the other to massage the sole with hacking movements. Finish with effleurage. Ask the receiver to turn over on to their back, and move to kneel by their feet.

Place your hands across the top of one ankle with fingers pointing away from each other. Anchor the foot with your knees. Effleurage up the leg, fanning your hands at the top of the thighs and gliding them smoothly down the sides. You can use alternating hands.

Raise the knee and knead the calf muscles with one hand; support the ankle with the other. With the knee still raised, use firm effleurage on the thighs, alternating hands. Rest the hand you are not using on the knee.

Use kneading, wringing and pummelling to work on any tense areas of the leg.

Lie the leg flat and work on the knees. Circle the knee cap with your thumbs and stroke up the side of the knee, letting your thumbs pass each other at the top. Use circling thumb pressure all over the knee and finish by gently stroking under the knee.

Finish with effleurage over the whole leg. On the last stroke hold the foot with both hands for a moment.

Feet

Foot massage is excellent for relaxation and for keeping feet flexible and healthy.

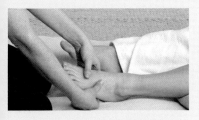

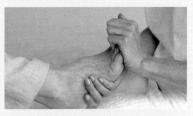

Use firm pressure and very little oil to avoid tickling. Start with effleurage with one hand on top of the foot and the other hand underneath. Support the foot with your fingers and use thumbs strokes over the top of the foot and in between the tendons.

Wiggle, squeeze and pull each of the toes in turn and finish by holding them all in one hand and gently pushing them backwards and forwards. Place your thumbs on the sole of the feet, fingers on the top and use thumb pressure over the sole. You can also use knuckling, circling pressure and hacking here.

Finish with effleurage and then hold the foot for a moment.

Hands

We do everything with our hands, so it should come as no surprise that they can become very tense.

A regular hand massage can be wonderfully relaxing. A simple hand massage is explained on page 40 but you might want to add a few stretches and some gentle thumb effleurage around the wrist.

Finish by stroking the whole hand and then sandwiching it between your own for a moment.

31

Arms

Massaging the arms can help with aching shoulders, headaches, neck pain and tired hands.

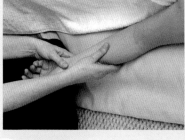

Lie the receiver on their back with hands resting palms down. Place both your hands together with fingers across the arm facing away from each other and effleurage from the top of the wrist to the shoulder, stroking firmly on the way up, lightly on the way down the sides of the arm. You can effleurage with one hand, holding the receiver's hand with the other.

Lift the forearm leaving the elbow resting on the floor. Support the wrist with one hand and slide the other firmly down to the elbow, pressing with your thumb, glide gently back up to the wrist. Then use both thumbs to stroke down the insides of the wrist to the inside of the elbow.

The forearm is often tense, so use firm kneading. Rest the forearm on your thigh if this is easier. While in this position use your fingers to circle around the elbow, and use thumb pressure over the elbow. You may need extra oil as the skin is often dry on the elbow.

Effleurage the upper arm and knead with one hand while supporting the upper arm with the other. Use wringing and squeezing too, but be careful not to pinch.

Finish with feathering over the whole arm and then hold the hand gently for a few moments. You can then move the whole arm up and down a few times and rotate from the shoulder, finishing with a gentle pull.

Abdomen

A gentle abdominal massage can help with stomach aches, indigestion, constipation and period pains.

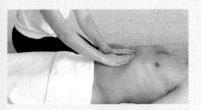

Kneel next to the abdomen and place your hands side by side, fingers pointing towards the head. Effleurage up to the ribs and down the sides.

Turn to face across the abdomen, rest your left hand on the ribs and use your right hand to circle gently clockwise around the navel.

Start circling with both hands. When your arms cross, lift your left hand over your right arm then place it on the abdomen; start circling again.

Apply gentle pressure around the navel using one hand on top of the other. Avoid deep pressure as this can be painful.

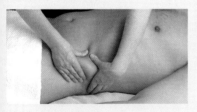

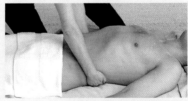

Knead the whole area, including the hips. Then with relaxed hands stroke slowly up the side of the waist, one hand following the other.

Place your hands on either side of the waist, pull up the sides and glide the hands smoothly across the abdomen. Finish with effleurage and feathering.

Cup a hand over the navel, trapping air underneath. Hold, feeling the heat gathering, then slowly flatten your hand as if to push the heat into the body. Relax your hands and very slowly lift them away, as if pulling the tension from the receiver's body.

Chest and neck

Bad posture makes the chest muscles tense, which in turn affects the shoulders, neck and upper back. This can lead to long-term problems, with difficulty in straightening and walking later in life. Massaging the chest helps with aches and pains in these areas.

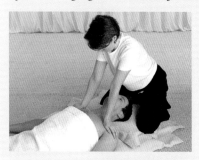

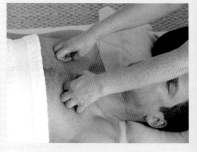

Kneel behind the head and place a hand on each shoulder with your fingers facing towards the floor. Lean into the shoulders to stretch and loosen the muscles.

Turn your hands so that the fingers face across the body. Effleurage around the chest, shoulders and back of the neck.

Use kneading, thumb pressure and knuckling on the upper chest, behind the shoulders and base of the neck.

Place your hands on each side of the neck in turn and stroke in towards the base of the skull using alternate hands, gently pushing the head from side to side. Then use both hands on one side of the neck, stroking with alternate hands from the shoulder. Repeat on the other side.

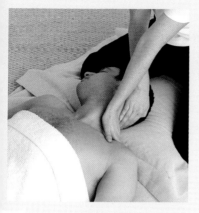

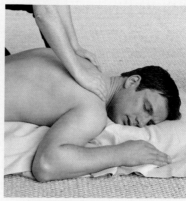

Put one hand on one shoulder and the other under the base of the skull on the same side. Push the shoulder down while pulling the head gently away from the neck to stretch the neck muscles. Repeat on the other side.

Ask the receiver to turn over to lie on their front. Using firm circular pressure with your two middle fingers on either side of the spine, work up the neck to the base of the skull, then work along the base of skull.

Finish by cupping your hands around the base of the skull and stretch gradually by leaning back slowly. Hold the head in both hands (one hand on the forehead, the other under the base of the skull) and turn the head from side to side and gently forward and back.

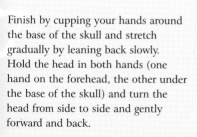

Face

A face massage can leave you looking (and feeling!) younger, more refreshed and healthier.

Kneel behind the head. Use a face oil or enriched face cream. To spread the cream or oil place both hands on the neck and use effleurage over the neck, up the chin, up the side of the face to the ears. Pause before gliding back down to the neck.

Use your finger tips to stroke from the chin, round the mouth and nostrils, up the side of the nose, across the cheekbones to the temples and back down to the chin. Then stroke up again as far as the forehead, pause here, apply a little pressure then glide down to the chin. Stroke under the neck from shoulders to ears with alternate hands. Then pat along the jawline with alternate hands.

Cup both hands over the face, fingers facing down the body and hold for a moment, press down gently then glide towards the ears and pause.

Use small upward circular movements with your fingertips to massage around the mouth and under the cheekbones.

Place your hands across the forehead, fingers touching, and stroke outwards using your fingers. Then turn your hand so that your fingers face down the body and stroke out with the sides of your thumbs towards the temples, finish each time by pressing gently on the temples.

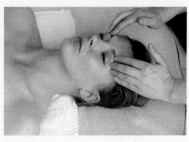

Use circular pressure over the whole forehead. Place one hand across the forehead and stroke up towards the hairline, as one hand finishes repeat the movement with the other hand.

Use your finger tips and press gently round the eye sockets and under the eyebrows, then place your fingers gently over the eyes, pause then glide towards the temples. Finish the routine by placing both hands over the face for a few moments.

Head

Massaging the thin layer of muscle covering the skull is a great way of alleviating anxiety and helping the receiver to relax.

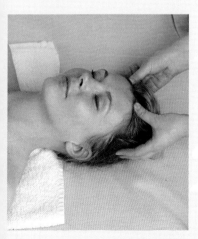

Make small circular movements over the whole scalp with your fingers, working from the front towards the back. Then gently stroke the hair. Take small bunches, pull gently and release, gliding your fingers through the hair as you do. Do this all over the scalp.

Bring both hands to rest behind the neck and gently pull the head towards you to stretch the neck. Finish by bringing your hands up over the ears, press in gently then slide the hands up and off the top of the head.

Simple neck and shoulder massage

This massage routine can be done through clothes, so it can be used anywhere, at any time.

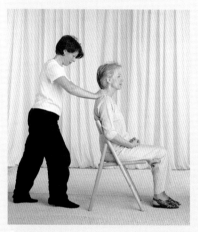

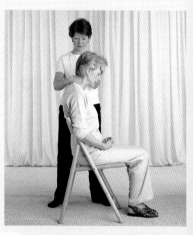

The receiver should sit in a comfortable chair that leaves the upper back and neck free.

Stand behind the chair and gently make contact with the receiver's shoulders using the heel of your hand. Push your hands into their shoulders and squeeze the muscles. Using your own body weight, lean your thumbs into the shoulder muscles between the spine and shoulder blades, and rotate your thumbs.

Hold the receiver's forehead in one hand and place the other hand on the back of their neck. Lean into and squeeze the neck muscles, including the base of the skull.

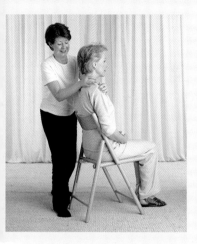

Move one arm so that it lies across the receiver's chest and supports them, and use the heel of your other hand to knead the upper back and shoulders. Increase the pressure exerted by leaning into the shoulders.

Gently rotate each arm. Stroke the receiver's forehead, head and down their back; and gently squeeze down each arm.

You can finish by resting your hands on the receiver's shoulders for a few moments, or by stroking down the receiver's arms and legs and holding the feet for a moment as a way of incorporating the rest of the body into the massage.

Simple hand massage

It may not always be possible to offer a full body massage, but a hand massage can be comforting and can be done anywhere. You can do this routine with or without oil depending on the receiver's preference. If you do use oil, remember to roll up the receiver's sleeves to avoid getting oil on their clothes. It is also a good idea to place a towel under their arm to prevent oil staining furniture.

Take one hand in both of yours and massage with your thumbs using gentle circular movements.

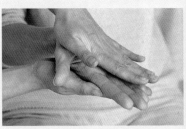

With the receiver's hand palm up resting in one of your hands, stroke the palm with the heel of your other hand. Lean your thumb into the area and circle over it.

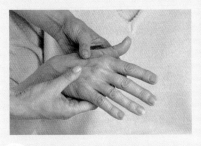

Turn the receiver's hand over and support it with your fingers while you stroke the back with your thumbs.

Squeeze between the bones and gently squeeze, wring and stretch each finger.

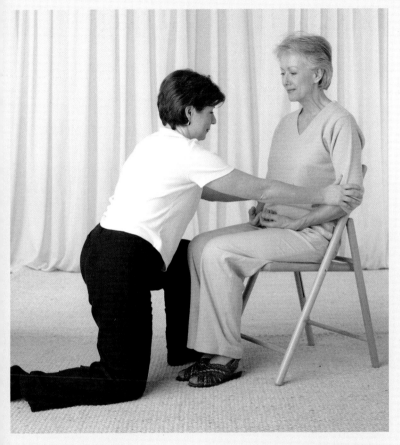

Complete the massage by gently stroking the receiver's shoulders, arms and hands.

SIMPLE FOOT MASSAGE

This hand massage can be adapted for the foot if the receiver prefers. Make sure you can sit comfortably without bending over, to avoid back strain.

Massage during pregnancy and childbirth

Going through pregnancy and childbirth is a life-changing experience, as well as being physically and emotionally demanding. Gentle massage can be enormously beneficial and may help sleeplessness and backache. Problems such as aching legs, cramps, fluid retention, mood swings and breast tenderness also respond well to massage.

The receiver will not be able to lie on her abdomen, so try one of the following positions instead:

- lying on side with the uppermost knee bent and resting on a pillow. Support her head with pillows.

- sitting astride a chair facing its back, leaning against a pillow or a folded duvet.

When lying on her back, make sure the receiver has pillows to prop her up and put a pillow under her knees.

The key is to use very gentle strokes and to spend more time on the legs, back and abdomen as these are often the areas that feel most uncomfortable.

If a doctor has advised against massaging any of these areas, a relaxing face massage and a simple foot and hand massage will still be very beneficial.

SAFETY TIPS

- do not massage if the receiver is in the first trimester or has a history of miscarriage
- check with the receiver's doctor that massage is safe
- avoid deep pressure strokes and tapotement
- avoid ankles, lower back and pelvic area unless cleared with the doctor
- do not massage if there are complications such as high blood pressure, diabetes, anaemia or vaginal bleeding
- check any essential oils used are safe during pregnancy

ABDOMEN

Kneel by the receiver and use gentle, clockwise effleurage around her abdomen, using first one hand and then both hands.

Effleurage up the sides of the waist with alternate hands. Lift your hands off as they reach the navel. Stroke up the abdomen and down the sides. Finish by gently resting both hands on top of the navel.

LEGS

Use effleurage between the ankle and the top of the thigh. Avoid direct massage of varicose veins.

ARMS

The woman can lie on her side or back. Support her arm with one hand as you gently effleurage with the other one.

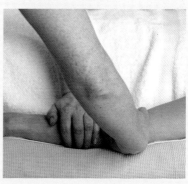

BACK

Use mainly effleurage movements, but do use some friction and squeezing around the shoulders and neck to help relieve tension.

MASSAGE DURING LABOUR

During childbirth, massage can help to relieve backache. It is also a wonderful way of supporting a partner and helping them relax. Massage the lower back with firm circular pressure, using the heel of your hands or your thumbs. Between contractions, a gentle face massage or a firm foot massage can be a relaxing distraction.

MASSAGE POSTNATALLY

Every new mother deserves regular massages. Caring for a new-born baby is exhausting, especially after the stresses of childbirth. Offer a full body massage and, if the mother's doctor gives permission, pay particular attention to the abdomen. Be gentle and do not massage a scar from a Caesarean section.

Baby massage

Baby massage is an ancient art practised in many traditional cultures, where it is seen as a natural part of child rearing. In the West touch is often an undervalued and neglected sense. While we cuddle and caress our children, we have only recently rediscovered the joys and benefits of baby massage.

Baby massage requires no special techniques. Stroking movements are the easiest to use, and where an area is too small for your whole hand, use fingertips and thumbs.

Start with your baby on their back so you can establish eye contact and trust. You should also talk to them reassuringly throughout. Babies have a short attention span so a 10-minute routine is probably enough.

Massage with a light vegetable oil such as almond oil or sunflower oil, and use smooth, slow movements. Warm the oil to body temperature beforehand and make sure your hands are warm too.

Make sure your baby is not hungry or too tired; about half an hour after a feed or after a bath are often good times. A large, soft towel over a changing mat on a table or on the floor makes a good massage space.

The room needs to be very warm and draught free, so a bathroom after a bath would be ideal.

SAFETY TIPS

- Avoid using essential oils unless you are very confident about possible risks.
- Do not leave your baby alone on a table as they can roll off. Collect everything you will need beforehand and make sure you will not be disturbed.
- Remember the same safety guidelines apply to babies as to adults.
- If your baby is not enjoying the massage – stop and try again later.

WHY BABY MASSAGE?

Benefits for both parent and baby:
- supports and builds strong bonds
- teaches both how to relax together
- gives quality time together

Benefits for baby:
- relaxation and enjoyment
- helps with sleep problems
- teaches the baby they are loved and valued
- develops body awareness, coordination, suppleness and alertness
- relief from irritability, teething, colic, constipation and congestion
- releases some of the trauma of a difficult birth
- strengthens and regulates immune, circulatory, respiratory, nervous, digestive and eliminatory systems

Benefits for parent:
- another opportunity to touch, pleasure and relaxation
- helps parent learn to read and respond appropriately to their baby's non-verbal and verbal communications
- increases confidence and parent's awareness of their baby's growth and development

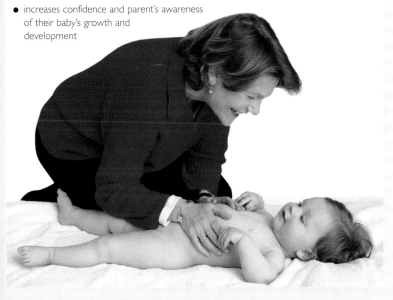

Face

With your baby on its back place your hands on each side of the face, then stroke the forehead from the centre outwards. Stroke from the nose to the temples and then down the sides of the face to the chin.

Using the tips of your fingers circle lightly round the baby's eyes. Stroke along the eyebrows to the temples and back under the eyes. Finish by pressing very gently on the baby's temples.

Arms and legs

Hold up one arm and stroke down from the shoulder, then gently squeeze all over. Hold your baby's hand while stroking the back of the hand. Gently squeeze and rotate each finger.

Use the same routine for legs and feet. At the end of the massage move the arms up and down and across the baby's chest, and bend and stretch the legs.

Abdomen

Place one hand on each thigh and effleurage up the front of your baby's body then over the shoulders, down the arms and the side of the body, then back to the thighs. Alternate your hands with one stroking upwards as the other glides smoothly down.

With one hand on each side of the abdomen and your fingers pointing towards each other, use a smooth criss-crossing movement, back and

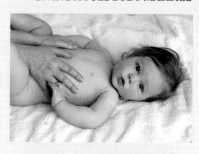

forth over the abdomen. Then stroke in a circular movement around the navel, with one hand following the other – this is particularly helpful for colicky babies.

Back

This can be difficult to do, as older babies try to roll over or crawl away. Make sure the head is turned to one side comfortably. Stroke from the backs of the legs, over the bottom and up over the back and shoulders, then gently down the baby's sides.

Use gently circling pressure with your thumbs up each side of the spine. Use criss-crossing movements over the back in a rhythmic motion.

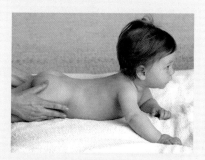

Stroke each buttock and knead gently. Babies also like gentle patting and pinching. Finish by gently stroking down the back with alternate hands.

MASSAGING CHILDREN

There is no reason to stop massaging your children as they get older. Pick a quiet time and offer a short massage – perhaps a back rub or a simple hand or foot massage. If children do not want to undress do not force them – you can massage through a T-shirt and pants.

47

Self

Mas

There are many times when everyday stresses get on top of us, but instead of letting the pressure build, a simple self-massage can set you back on course.

Self-massage is something anyone can do. You probably use a form of it already when you rub a stiff neck or massage your temples. The techniques described here simply formalize what we do instinctively when a part of our body hurts, is tense or stiff. This section will:

- explain some simple and quick self-massage techniques
- describe two self-massage routines for headaches and backache

Massage

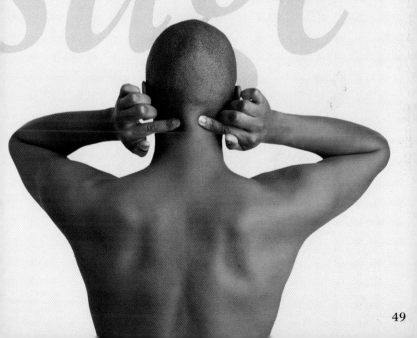

Self-massage techniques

BACK

Sit on the edge of a bed or stool and press your thumbs into the dimples on either side of your lower spine.

Use circling thumb pressure and knuckling on tense areas. Effleurage to relax and soothe.

ABDOMEN

Lie on your back with knees bent up and feet apart. Place your hands on top of each other on your navel. Make large, clockwise, circular movements. Try kneading with fingers and thumbs. Finish with effleurage.

LEGS

Sit on the floor and effleurage over your leg from
the foot up. Then knead the thigh. Effleurage, then
pummel front and outside of thigh.

  Massage around your knee with your fingers,
using circular pressure. Finish with gentle upward
strokes behind your knee.

  Lastly knead your calf muscles
with both hands, and finish
with effleurage.

FEET

Sit on the floor resting one foot on the opposite
thigh. Put one hand over the top of the foot,
the other underneath, then effleurage.

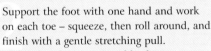

Support the foot with one hand and work
on each toe – squeeze, then roll around, and
finish with a gentle stretching pull.

  Use thumb pressure and hacking on your
soles. Finish with effleurage.

HANDS

1 Effleurage the back of one hand firmly towards the wrist, and gently back. Squeeze your hand all over by pressing it between your fingers and palm.

2 Massage each finger using the toe sequence. Use thumb pressure on your palms and finish with effleurage.

ARMS

1 Effleurage firmly from shoulder to wrist, with gentle strokes downwards. Knead up the arm and use circular thumb pressure on your forearm.

2 Use gentle cupping to stimulate and finish with effleurage.

FACE

Place your hands over your face with the fingers on your forehead and the heels of the hands on your chin. Hold for a moment, then gently draw the hands towards your ears. While you are doing this, imagine that you are drawing the tension away from your face.

Place your hands on your forehead with your fingertips facing each other and use gentle strokes outwards. Repeat on your cheeks and chin.

Pinch along your jawline using your thumb and knuckle of your index fingers, then, alternating your hands, gently slap under your chin with the backs of your hands. Keep your tongue curled back while doing this.

Gently press around your eye sockets with your thumbs, then close your eyes and stroke the lids. Make an 'O' shape with your mouth and apply small circular pressure movements around the mouth with your fingers.

Use your fingertips to apply small circular movements over your scalp. Finish by pressing gently but firmly on your temples.

NECK AND SHOULDERS

Sit on a chair and relax your neck forwards. Clasp your hands together behind your head and use your thumbs to effleurage firmly downwards. Then apply circular finger pressure to the base of the skull.

Cross your arms over your chest and use your right hand to apply deep finger pressure to your left shoulder blade. Then use your left hand on your right shoulder blade.

Uncross your arms and finish by stroking up firmly from your collar bone to your chin with the back of your hand.

SELF-MASSAGE FOR BACKACHE

Lie on your back and bring your knees up to your chest, then gently rock backwards and forwards for one minute.

Sit up and press your fingers firmly into the top of your buttocks, pushing them into the flesh four times. Repeat this technique all round the top of your buttocks and on either side of your lower spine.

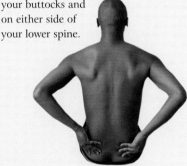

SELF-MASSAGE FOR HEADACHES

Sit with your back supported and both feet on the ground. Press your index fingers into the bottom of the occipital bone at the base of your head and hold for a few seconds, repeat three times.

With the same fingers, use gentle circular movements on the temples in both directions.

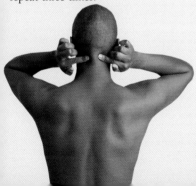

Using
Essential
FOR

The use of essential oils is a wonderfully sensuous addition to massage. Not only can the fragrances lift your mood but the individual oils have therapeutic properties that can enhance the health-giving effect of massage. This section will:

- explain the principles of aromatherapy
- offer safety tips
- advise on choosing, buying, and storing essential oils
- describe commonly used essential oils
- provide useful oil combinations for common problems

Oils
Massage

What is aromatherapy?

We seem to know instinctively that aroma is important to health, and since ancient times aromatics have been incorporated into medicines and beauty preparations. We have learnt how to extract essential oils from leaves, petals, bark, seeds, stalks and flowers and discovered that essential oils have therapeutic properties.

Essential oils are readily absorbed through the skin and interact with our bodies in the following ways:

- pharmacologically through chemical changes when they enter the bloodstream
- physiologically by producing a physical effect on the body such as sedation or stimulation
- psychologically, when the aroma of an oil is inhaled and we react positively or negatively.

Aromatherapy is the therapeutic use of these specially-prepared essential oils. It was a French chemist called René-Maurice Gattefosse who coined the term in 1928. He had discovered, by chance, that lavender essential oil was an effective treatment for burns, and, as a result, went on to discover the therapeutic properties of other essential oils.

Today, there are about 300 different essential oils in use but in the home only a handful are needed for everyday uses.

Aromatherapy is a useful complement to other therapies, helping to enhance our sense of well-being and relieve stress and stress-related problems.

Using essential oils

There are many ways in which essential oils can be applied. The most common method is through massage, where small amounts of essential oils are added to the base or carrier oil.

Essential oils can be added to skin oils and lotions such as cold creams, which are applied with gentle circular movements so as not to pull the skin.

Up to eight drops of an essential oil or combination of oils can be added to a full bath – after the temperature has been adjusted. Oils are added to compresses to relieve pain or inflammation, to steam inhalations for the relief of respiratory problems, and to spring water to make flower waters. Essential oils may also be used in special burners.

Essential oil safety

Essential oils are concentrated and should be used with care. With a few exceptions (e.g. lavender) they should not be applied to the skin undiluted. For massage, generally use 1–2 drops to 5 ml (1 tsp) base oil, and for a full body massage, 10–20 ml (2–4 tsp) of base oil. Never take oils internally and keep them out of the reach of children.

Many oils can make the skin more sensitive to ultraviolet light, especially bergamot, lemon, orange, lemon verbena, lime and cumin, so avoid strong sunlight after using them.

Some oils irritate the skin, so use with care, and not at all if the receiver has skin or allergy problems. These include basil, lemon, lemongrass, lemon verbena, melissa, peppermint, thyme and sweet fennel, amongst others.

Sweet fennel and rosemary essential oils should not be used for anyone with epilepsy, and rosemary, sage and thyme should not be used if a receiver has high blood pressure.

Arnica, basil, clary sage and cypress, amongst others should never be used during pregnancy. Sweet fennel and rosemary should not be used in the first trimester, and after that only if well diluted. Avoid using chamomile and lavender if there is a risk of miscarriage or abnormal bleeding.

To avoid allergic reactions you can do a patch test. Blend a small amount of essential oil with a base oil and apply to the skin. If you or the receiver reacts with itchiness, blistering or any other allergic reaction, avoid using this oil.

BUYING AND STORING ESSENTIAL OILS

Essential oils vary in price and quality. It is important that any oil you buy is pure. Blended oils are cheaper but they have been mixed with chemicals. A pure oil is never mixed and comes from a named botanical plant from a definite geographical area.

Some oils are marketed as aromatherapy oils – cheaper mixtures of essential and carrier oils. The proportion of essential oil varies but may be as little as 4 per cent.

Many aromatherapists recommend using essential oils distilled from organically grown plants but there is little regulation governing this and no guarantee of quality.

Essential oils should be stored in tightly closed, dark glass bottles in a cool cupboard, away from heat and light, as they deteriorate in sunlight and evaporate in the air. Some oils, such as jasmine and neroli, should be kept in the fridge. The therapeutic effects of most oils will last for two to three years, although citrus oils last for only a year.

17 essential oils and their properties

Bergamot (Citrus bergamia)
The fresh citrusy aroma of this oil lifts the spirits and is used for stress, anxiety and depression. Also: eczema, dermatitis, respiratory, urinary and digestive problems.

Chamomile, Roman (Anthemis nobilis)
Soothing and gentle, this oil is particularly helpful with infant problems such as colic. Also gives relief from migraine, insomnia and stress, as well as skin problems, inflammatory disorders and menstrual problems.

Clary Sage (Salvia sclarea)
Regarded by some as the most euphoric of all essential oils, clary sage helps release emotions and inhibitions and boosts libidos. It can also help with depression, relaxation, relief of menstrual pains and premenstrual stress.

Eucalyptus (Eucalyptus globulus)
One of the most commonly used of essential oils, eucalyptus is best known as a treatment for colds, flu, bronchitis, mucus congestion and sinusitis. It can also help with rheumatism and arthritis, cystitis and other urinary and skin infections; and it makes an effective insect repellent.

Geranium (Pelargonium graveolens)
This balancing oil affects the mind and body. It is refreshing, uplifting and centring and helps with anxiety, depression, and to diffuse defensive feelings towards others. Premenstrual tension and skin disorders also respond well to geranium.

Jasmine (Jasminum officinale)
Called the 'king of essential oils', pure jasmine oil is expensive. Its heady scent is sensuous and is used for sexual difficulties. It is also helpful in depression, in labour to promote contractions, postnatally to avoid post-natal depression, and for skin problems.

Juniper (Juniperus communis)
This stimulating and cleansing oil is used to help rid the mind of negative thoughts, encourage self confidence and resolve, for urinary tract infections and fluid retention.

Lavender (Lavandula angustifolia)
This is undoubtedly the most popular essential oil, and certainly one of the most versatile. Lavender's evocative scent is soothing, balancing and nurturing. It is excellent for stress and tension, headaches, pain relief, and for many infections. It is widely used in skin preparations.

Lemongrass (Cymbopogon citratus)
This oil has a wonderfully uplifting aroma and is used to combat nervous tension, lethargy, mild digestive problems, and aches and pains.

Marjoram (Origanum marjorana)
This is an effective oil if you feel tired and are aching. It is also good for lack of sleep, stress, migraine and diarrhoea.

Neroli (Citrus aurantium)
Another expensive oil, neroli – from orange blossom – is beneficial for all stress-related problems, nervous tension and as an aphrodisiac.

Orange (Citrus aurantium)
Orange oil helps to clear sluggish systems, such as the liver, and alleviates slow digestion, tension headaches and tiredness.

Parsley (Petroselinum sativum/crispum)
The oil smells more bitter than the fresh plant, useful for premenstrual tension, cystitis and painful periods, as well as the treatment of broken capillaries and bruises.

Rose (Rosa centifolia)
The red petals from 30 blooms are needed to produce just one drop of this oil. Its exquisite aroma has a profound effect on the emotions, being particularly helpful for depression, grief, jealousy, resentment and shock.

Rosemary (Rosmarinus officinalis)
This energizing oil stimulates mental activity, concentration and memory. Rosemary is highly recommended for pain relief in muscles and joints, for alleviating digestive and circulation problems, and for easing headaches.

Sandalwood (Santalum album)
Sensually stirring, sandalwood balances, gently soothing away anxiety and tension, encouraging communication and feelings of peace and tranquillity. It is helpful with phobias, including sexual problems and fears, and is added to many skin preparations.

Thyme (Thymus vulgaris)
Thyme is used to help with rheumatism, sciatica and muscular pains, tiredness and depression, skin problems and irritation and for infectious diseases. It also acts as an effective expectorant.

Ylang Ylang (Cananga odorata)
The scent of this oil is sweet and intoxicating, exotic and erotic. A sedative oil, it is useful for stress and insomnia, and also for relieving high blood pressure. It calms anxiety while boosting energy, and is widely used in skin preparations and perfumes.

COMBINING ESSENTIAL OILS FOR HEALTH

Essential oils can be used in combination to maximize their therapeutic effect in massage. Once mixed with a base oil, these combinations will keep for around three months.

FOR RELAXATION

3 drops bergamot
2 drops sandalwood
1 drop geranium
20 ml (4 tsp) pure vegetable oil
This combination helps reduce tension,
anxiety, and insomnia. It can be used in a
whole body massage, a neck and shoulder massage,
or a simple back massage.

FOR ACHES AND PAINS

3 drops rosemary
3 drops juniper
2 drops lemongrass
20 ml (4 tsp) pure vegetable oil
This helps with muscular aches and pains, sprained
or arthritic joints, and before or after exercise.

FOR HEADACHES

1 drop lavender or 1 drop rosemary
5 ml (1 tsp) grapeseed oil
Massage around back of neck, temples and eyes.

FOR LIFTING THE SPIRITS

1 drop marjoram, neroli or thyme
5 ml (1 tsp) grapeseed oil
Massage on the back of the hand, stomach and solar plexus.

FOR PREMENSTRUAL TENSION

4 drops parsley
3 drops neroli
20 ml (4 tsp) soya oil
Massage into abdomen, lower back and back of neck.

Useful Contacts

The following organizations will supply you with information and equipment for massage:

In the UK
Aromatherapy Organisations Council
PO Box 19834
London SE25 6WF
Tel: 44 (0)20 8251 7912
Fax: 44 (0)20 8251 7942
www.aromatherapy-uk.org

British Massage Therapy Council
17 Rymers Lane
Oxford OX4 3JU
Tel: 44 (0)1865 774123
Fax: 44 (0)1865 774123
www.bmtc.co.uk

British Federation of Massage Practitioners
78 Meadow Street
Preston PR1 1TS
Tel: 44 (0)1772 881063
Fax: 44 (0)1772 881063

British Complementary Medicine Association
Kensington House
33 Imperial Square, Cheltenham
Gloucestershire GL50 1QZ
Tel: 44 (0)1242 519911

In Australia
Massage Academy
Suite 303, 282 Victoria Avenue,
Chatswood, 2067 NSW
Tel: 61 (0) 2 9410 2655

In Canada
Canadian College of Massage and Hydrotherapy
North York Campus
5160 Yonge Street
North York, Ontario. M2N 6L9
Tel: 1 416 250 8690

Canadian Massage Therapist Alliance
365 Bloor Street East, Suite 1807
Toronto, Ontario, M4W 3L4
Tel: 1 416 968 2149
Fax: 1 416 968 6818

In America
American Inst. of Massage Therapy, Inc.
2101 North, Federal Highway
Fort Lauderdale, Florida 33305
Tel: 1 954 568 6200
Fax: 1 954 568 6100
www.aimt.com/

San Francisco School of Massage
1327 Chestnut Street, Suites A & B
San Francisco, California 94123
Tel: 1 415 474 4600
www.sfsm.net

Index